FAVORITE HEBREW

For Voice & Piano

arranged by Albert Rozin

tara publications

FOREWORD

Albert Rozin was a well-known teacher of piano and organ as well as a noted composer of educational and liturgical music. He is also the author of the popular collection HEBREW FESTIVAL MELODIES.

This volume contains favorite Israeli, Hassidic and liturgical songs as well as selections for the Sabbath and Festivals. The arranger has created sensitive settings which are easy to play but which do not sacrifice the flavor of the original harmonies. Organists and guitar players will find little difficulty in playing the songs harmonically by using the chord symbols indicated in the music.

We hope that these songs will bring pleasure and joy to all who play them.

TARA PUBLICATIONS

Hatikvah

HEBREW NATIONAL ANTHEM

Od Yishama

Rabbi S. Carlebach

Od Yishama II

Siman Tov

Si-man tov u-ma-zal tov u-ma-zal tov v'-si-man tov si-man tov u-ma-zal tov u-

ma-zal tov v'-si-man tov si-man tov u-ma-zal tov u-ma-zal tov v'-si-man tov

y'-he la - nu y'-he la - nu

u - l'-chol Yis-ra - el

y' - he la - nu y'-he la - nu

u - l'-chol Yis-ra - el

v'-he la - nu y'-he la-nu

Hebraic Dance-Hashivenu

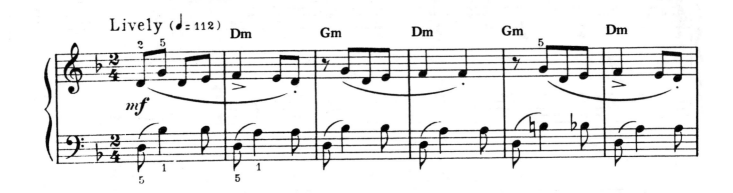

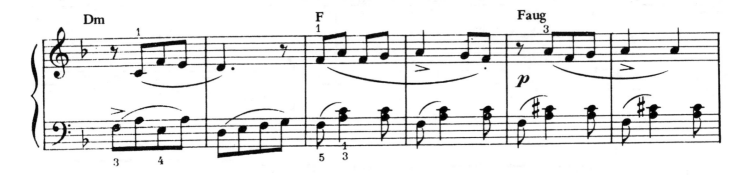

2nd time both hands one octave higher

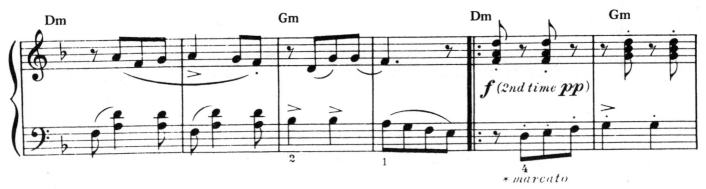

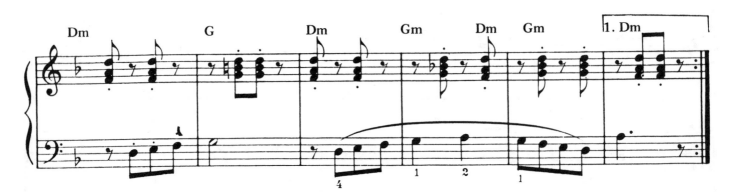

★ May be played in octaves the first time.

Hava Nagila

Come, brethren, let us sing and be gay.

Zum Gali

DUET

The pioneer is meant for work!
The work is meant for the pioneer!

ISRAELI TUNE

This song may be played as a solo by playing the Secondo part with the left hand.

Zum Gali

DUET

The pioneer is meant for work!
Work is meant for the pioneer!

ISRAELI TUNE

*The Secondo part may be taught by rote.

Hevenu Shalom Alechem

We bring you greetings of peace.

Hiney Ma Tov

How good and how pleasant it is
for brethren to dwell together.

FOLK SONG

Achshav

*Home at last in Emek Yisrael. Tumba,
tumba, tumba, in Emek Yisrael.*

Artza Alinu

We are ascending to our land.

SONG OF ISRAEL

Ar-tza a-li-nu, ar-tza a-li-nu, ar-tza a-li - nu.

Ar-tza a-li-nu, ar-tza a-li-nu, ar-tza a-li - nu.

K'var ḥa-rash-nu v'-gam za-ra - nu, k'var ḥa-rash-nu v'-gam za-ra - nu,

A-val od lo ka-tzar - nu, A-val od lo ka-tzar - nu,

A-val od lo ka-tzar - nu, A-val od lo ka-tzar - nu.

Yesh Lanu Koach

*Our faith is our strength. Together shall we
go up to Zion to rebuild our land.*

Ya Hai Li Li

Arise, brethren, to your labors! The world
depends on work. Our life is our work.

YEMENITE MELODY

Kum Bachur Atzel

Get up, lazy one and go to work.
Kukuriku, kukuriku, hear the rooster's call.

ISRAELI SONG AND DANCE

Shalom Chaverim

Farewell comrades, farewell. Until we meet again.

FOLK SONG

Sha - lom cha-ve -rim, sha - lom cha-ve -rim, sha - lom, sha -

lom. L' - hit - ra - ot, l' - hit - ra - ot, sha -

lom, sha - lom. Sha - lom cha-ve -rim, sha -

lom cha-ve -rim, sha - lom, sha - lom. L' -

hit - ra - ot, l' - hit - ra - ot, sha - lom, sha - lom.

Shabat Hamalka

The Sabbath has come with peace and joy.

CH. N. BIALIK
English Translation
by A. Irma Cohen

P. MINKOWSKI

Slowly, peacefully

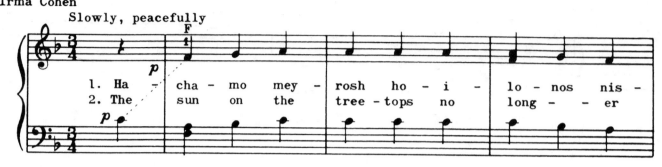

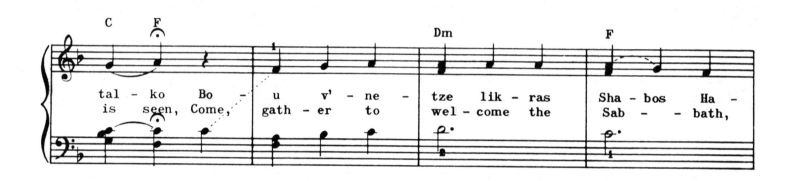

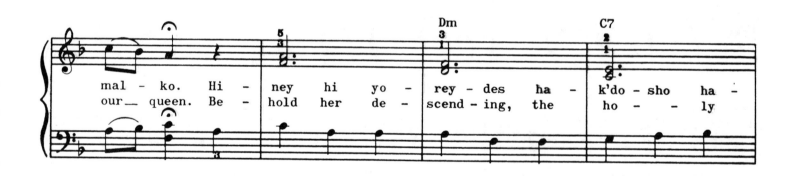

1. Ha - cha - mo mey - rosh ho - i - lo - nos nis - tal - ko Bo - u v' - ne - tze lik - ras Sha - bos Ha - mal - ko. Hi - ney hi yo - rey - des ha - k'do - sho ha - bru - cho, V' - i - mo mal - o - chim tz'vo sho - lom u -

2. The sun on the tree - tops no long - er is seen, Come, gath - er to wel - come the Sab - bath, our queen. Be - hold her de - scend - ing, the ho - ly the blest, And with her the an - gels of peace and

mnu - cho. Bo - i, bo - i ha - mal -
of rest. Draw near, 0 Queen and here___ a -

ko. Bo - i, bo - i ha - ka -
bide. Draw near, draw near, 0 Sab - bath

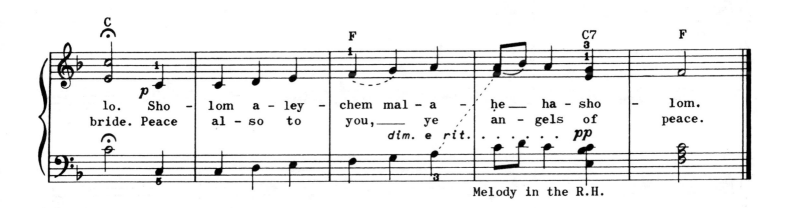

lo. Sho - lom a - ley - chem mal - a - he__ ha - sho - lom.
bride. Peace al - so to you,___ ye an - gels of peace.

Melody in the R.H.

3. We've welcomed the Sabbath with song and with prayer;

And home we return, our heart's gladness to share.

The table is set and the candles are lit,

The tiniest corner for Sabbath made fit.

O day of blessing, day of rest!

Sweet day of peace be ever blest!

Bring ye also peace, ye angels of peace.

Hashivenu

Restore us unto You and we shall be restored.
Renew our days of old.

CHASIDIC MELODY

V'taher Libenu

Purify our hearts that we may worship you in truth.

CHASIDIC MELODY

Joyously

V' – ta – her li-be –nu, v' ta – her li-be –nu, v'–

ta – her li-be – nu l' av-d'cha be – e –met, V' – av-d'cha be – e –met. *Fine*

La la la la (etc.) . . .

rit. . .

V' –
D.C. al Fine

Etz Chayim Hi

It is a tree of life to them that hold fast to it,
and everyone that upholds it is happy.

LITURGY

TRADITIONAL

Ovinu Malkenu

Our Father, Our King, be merciful to us.
Deal with us in kindness. Save us.

CHASIDIC MELODY

Kol Nidre

TRADITIONAL YOM KIPPUR PRAYER

Ono Adonoi

Save us, answer us, O Lord. O mighty
Redeemer, when we call to You.

TRADITIONAL

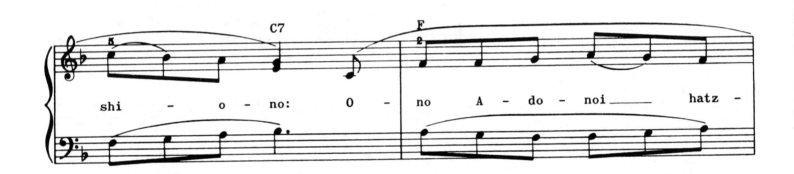

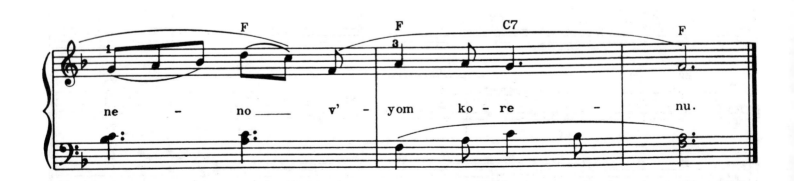

Chanukah

Chanukah is a festival of joy; Spin little dreydl, spin, spin, spin.

FOLK SONG

Cha - nu - ka, Cha - nu - ka, chag ya fe kol kach.

Or cha - viv mi - sa - viv gil l' - ye - led rach.

Cha - nu - ka, Cha - nu - ka, s' - vi - von sov, sov.

Sov, sov, sov, Sov, sov, sov, Mah - na im va - tov.

Mi Y'malel

Who can retell the things that befell us? Who can recount them?
In every age, a hero or sage arose to our aid.

CHANUKA SONG

Chag Purim

(Purim Day)

Purim is a day of joy, a day of gifts, masks and groggers.

FOLK SONG

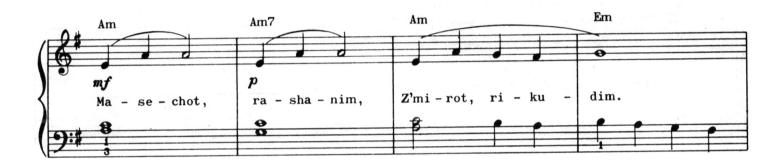

Utzu Etza

You may scheme and plot against us, but to no avail. For God is with us.

FOLK SONG

U – tzu e – tza ve' – tu – far,

U – tzu e – tza ve – tu – far,

U – tzu e – tza ve – tu – far,___ Dab – ru da – var ve – lo ya – kum,

Ki i – ma – nu ___ El. ___ U – tzu e – tza ve – tu – far,___

Hin'ni Muchan

Behold, I am prepared to sanctify the Sabbath, as is written in the Torah.

CHASIDIC MELODY

Dayenu

It would have been sufficient.

HAGADAH

FOLK SONG

I - lu - ho - tzi, ho - tzi - o - nu,   ho - tzi - o - nu mi - Mitz - ra - yim,

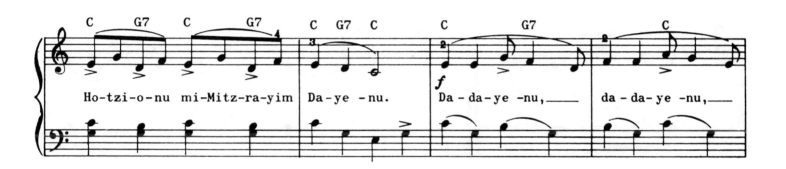

Ho - tzi - o - nu mi - Mitz - ra - yim Da - ye - nu.   Da - da - ye - nu,____ da - da - ye - nu,____

da - da ye - nu,   da ye - nu, da - ye - nu.   Da - da - ye - nu,____

da - da - ye - nu,____   da - da - ye - nu,   da - ye - nu, da - ye - nu.

L'shana Haba'a

Next year may we be in Jerusalem.

HAGADAH

MOSHE NATHANSON

Chad Gadyo

An only kid, my father bought for two zuzim.

HAGADAH   TRADITIONAL

Dundai

Israel and the Torah are one. Torah is light. Hallelujah.

FOLK SONG

2. Yalde Yisrael

limdu Torah

Hazku amtzu

nishmat hauma!

Tanu Rabanan

*Our saintly rabbis all agree to give praise and thanksgiving
to God, by whose divine decree all blessings we are receiving.*

FOLK SONG

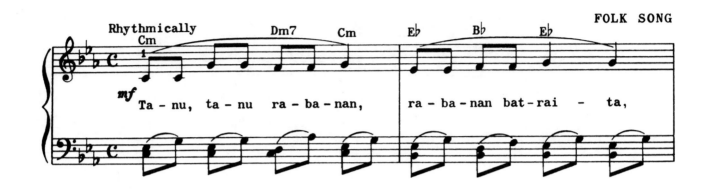

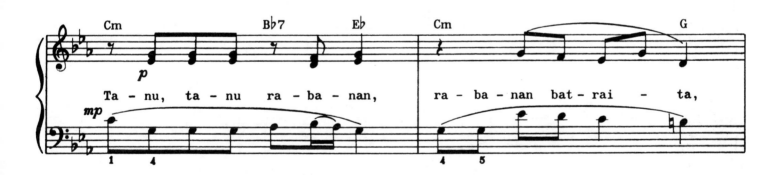

Yisrael V'oraita

Israel and the Torah are one. Torah is the light, hallelujah.

CHASIDIC MELODY

Ani Ma'amin

I believe with complete faith in the coming of the Messiah. And
though he may tarry, yet will I believe and await his coming.

LITURGY

FOLK SONG

Omar Rabbi Akivo

So Said Rabbi Akiva: Love your neighbor as yourself.

FOLK TUNE

Am Yisrael Chai

Israel lives forever!

FOLK SONG

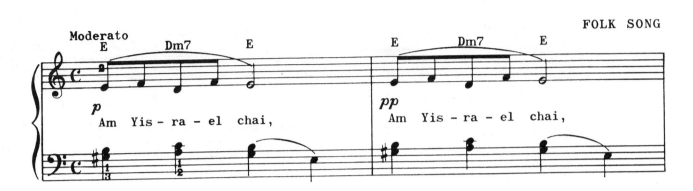

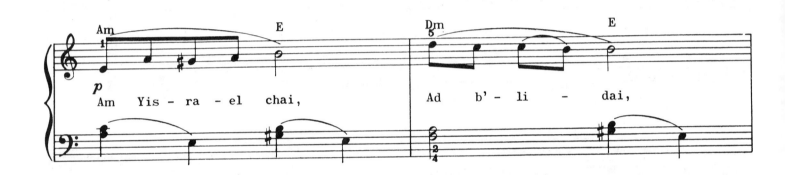

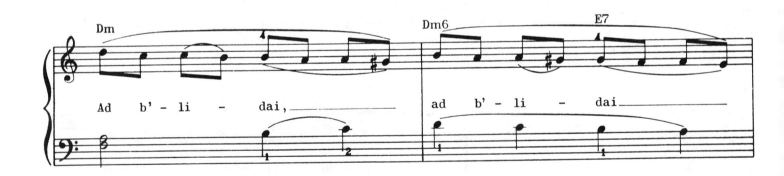

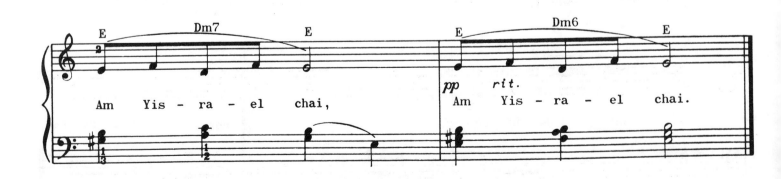